# HOW TO DELIVER
# A TED TALK

ISBN: 1468179993
ISBN 13: 9781468179996

# CONTENTS

# CHAPTER 1

# SPREAD YOUR IDEAS

If you are an avid viewer of TED videos, then you probably remember what it was like to watch your first TED video. Eighteen minutes of pure inspiration. TED's mission is to share ideas worth spreading and its missionaries do not disappoint. Though not household names, Sir Ken Robinson, Jill Bolte Taylor, and a thousand others, mesmerize their growing audience with powerful content, delivery, and design.

In the unlikely event that you have not yet watched one of their videos, TED is a nonprofit organization devoted to amplifying electrifying ideas from the domains of technology, entertainment, and design. Though TED has a variety of ventures, the two most notable are their highly exclusive conferences and their highly inclusive practice of posting presentations for free online.

If you have watched enough TED videos, you will notice that two distinctly different types of presenters grace the stage. People with amazing jobs or remarkable talents comprise the first type. The second type is people just like you and me who share their amazing stories.

Individuals such as Pranav Mistry and David Gallo inhabit the amazing jobs category. Marine biologist Gallo captivates his audience with visually astonishing creatures from ten thousand leagues under the sea. Mistry, a MIT Media Labs genius, gives us a peek into the future of how we will interact with data in the physical world. His SixthSense technology, consisting of a wearable camera and projector connected to a Smartphone, allows people to create a telephone keypad on their palm and to materialize and interact with the Internet on any surface. Written words cannot do justice to how revolutionary this technology is, so I encourage you to experience his TEDTalk online.

Remarkable talents can get you onto the TED stage as well. Two noteworthy examples are Arthur Benjamin performing his 'Mathemagic' tricks and Jake Shimabukuro's spellbinding rendition of Queen's Bohemian Rhapsody on the ukulele. One could never imagine that such amazing sounds could come out of an instrument that looks like a child's guitar with only four strings.

Few of us have had the fortune to land jobs that provoke the envy of our friends. Fewer still have dedicated their lives to a single talent and invested the thousands of hours required to achieve mastery. So, where does that leave the rest of us? How can we make it to the TED stage and inspire the world with our words?

The second type of TED presenters are just like you and me - ordinary individuals with extraordinary stories. Your first reaction may be defeatist. "I don't have an amazing story. My life is boring and 'normal.' I'm not a brain researcher who was able to study her own stroke like Jill Bolte Taylor. I did not grow up in Africa and become a celebrated writer like Nigerian novelist Chimamanda Adichie."

If you survived into adulthood, then you have countless stories of perseverance in the face of failure. You have loved and you have lost. You have harmed and you have been harmed. Ordinary lives are punctuated by extraordinary moments. Your stories can inspire others; you just need to learn to share them with full emotional force.

The problem is not that you do not have enough stories, it is that you have too many. Jill Bolte Taylor did not emerge from the womb as a brain researcher on one day, have a stroke on day two, and then get invited onto the TED stage on day three. She had thousands of remarkable experiences, but chose to talk about only one. This book will help you pick one remarkable idea and teach you how to share it in an inspiring way.

The TED conference organizers share a set of Ten Commandments with their invited speakers. Though these guidelines do offer a number of compelling best practices, they do not reveal how to give a TEDTalk. I have grouped the ten items into two categories below covering content and delivery:

- **Content**
  - » Thou Shalt Not Simply Trot Out Thy Usual Shtick.
  - » Thou Shalt Dream a Great Dream, or Show Forth a Wondrous New Thing, or Share Something Thou Hast Never Shared Before.
  - » Thou Shalt Tell a Story.
  - » Thou Shalt Not Sell from the Stage: Neither Thy Company, Thy Goods, Thy Writings, nor Thy Desperate Need for Funding; Lest Thou be Cast Aside into Utter Darkness.

» Thou Shalt Remember All the While: Laughter is Good.

- **Delivery**
  » Thou Shalt Reveal Thy Curiosity and Thy Passion.
  » Thou Shalt Freely Comment on the Utterances of Other Speakers for the Sake of Blessed Connection and Exquisite Controversy.
  » Thou Shalt Not Flaunt Thine Ego. Be Thou Vulnerable. Speak of Thy Failure as well as Thy Success.
  » Thou Shalt Not Read Thy Speech.
  » Thou Shalt Not Steal the Time of Them that Follow Thee.

The pages that follow provide a "how-to" guide for delivering an inspiring speech based on intensive study of the most popular TEDTalks. In step-by-step fashion, you will learn how to select a topic, craft a narrative, master delivery, and refine design.

*Note: In adherence with the "fair use" rule of United States copyright law, this book makes limited use of copyrighted excerpts from TED Conferences LLC for the purpose of criticism and commentary and for the purpose of providing a public good by elevating the presentation skills of aspiring speakers. Though I have no affiliation with TED, it is my hope that this book significantly increases the number of people exposed to the organization and their mission. All company and product names mentioned herein are the trademarks or registered trademarks of their respective owners.*

# PART-I

# CONTENT, STORY, & STRUCTURE

# CHAPTER 2

# HOW TO SELECT YOUR TOPIC

To create a compelling TEDTalk, you need to begin with the end in mind. After each audience member leaves the auditorium or surfs on to the next website, you must have planted one seed that either awakens their consciousness to a new way of thinking or persuades them to take action. Your objective is to sow a single seed of inspiration.

Selecting a topic requires an act of deep introspection. Although stories are the centerpiece of every TEDTalk, asking 'What is the most amazing story I can tell?' is the wrong question. Instead, begin by asking questions of self-discovery such as: What is the greatest lesson I ever learned? What is the greatest joy I ever experienced? The greatest misery? What is my life's mission and how can I enlist others to join my crusade?

Once you have your central idea, work backward to build an audience-centric narrative with layers of stories and facts. Imagine you chose to share the greatest lesson you ever learned. Your story becomes how and when you learned it. Most importantly, your talk should include from whom you learned the lesson since the most inspiring stories position someone else as the hero. As you build out your talk, constantly play the role of a skeptical listener asking "So what?" and "What is in it for me?"

Of the ten most viewed TEDTalks as of the end of 2011, seven focused on inspiring people to change themselves. There is no novelty in the concepts they address; there is nothing new under the sun. (Case in point, that expression is a two thousand year old biblical quote from Ecclesiastes.) Those seven focused on concepts inside the human mind including: mental illness, creativity, leadership, happiness, motivation, success, and self-worth.

The other three most viewed TEDTalks cast a wider net by catalyzing interpersonal and societal change. They called us to action or altered our perspective on public health, public education, and diversity. The speakers who gave these talks were not the first to explore those subjects and they will not be the last. They touched us by giving their perspective on why these ideas matter and how you can make a difference.

As you think about making emotional connections that inspire your audience, keep in mind that people generally have four deep rooted needs that emerge after we have met our needs for physiological health and physical security.

The first of the four is the need for love and belonging. In mid 2011, Gerda Grimshaw posted the question "What makes you happy?" on the TED discussion group on LinkedIn. Gerda is founder of Call Mom, a free referral service that connects single mothers and their children with resources and education to help them become self-sufficient and to thrive. Of the more than 100 responses generated, 92 of them were people genuinely sharing the source of their happiness. Though my approach was not unimpeachably scientific, I classified and categorized the responses to understand the secret behind contentment. As you can see from the following list, love and belonging, expressed via social interaction, dominates the list:

- Social interaction with family, friends, and yes, pets (30.4%)

- Experiencing nature (12.0%)

- Charity & volunteering (10.9%)

- Task completion (9.8%)

- Inspiring others though coaching, teaching, or writing (7.6%)

- Introspection & learning (7.6%)

- Mindfulness or "being in the moment" (6.5%)

- Health – particularly among people with recent or chronic illness (5.4%)

- Physical pleasure & exercise (5.4%)

- Self expression (2.2%)

- Financial well being (2.2%)

The second of the fundamental deep rooted needs is desire and self-interest. In the above list, physical pleasure and exercise as well as financial well being fall into this group. Truth be told, the frequency of these items in the general population is probably a bit higher, but it is socially taboo to comment on these desires in LinkedIn's mostly squeaky clean and not anonymous discussion groups. Lest you think such subjects are not the stuff of TEDTalks, think again. Mary Roach shared "10 Things You Did Not Know About Orgasm" in her TED2009 presentation and Helen Fisher revealed "Why We Love + Cheat" in her TED2006 performance. There are plenty of talks on money too, albeit with a slant toward inspiring people to overcome their inhibitions and pursue their entrepreneurial dreams.

Accelerating personal development is the third fundamental need that you can access to connect with your audience. We all want to learn and to grow. We are curious about ourselves and we work to challenge and ultimately overcome our limitations. We are equally curious about the world around us. By way of example, if you have a recipe for setting and achieving goals, then you have the makings of a great TEDTalk. The mechanics of this kind of topic are oft-used; what is novel is the story of how you have failed, learned, and overcome adversity.

It is no accident that "Hope and Change" was the centerpiece of Barack Obama's 2008 presidential campaign. It is the centerpiece of every mass movement, be it social, political, or religious. And, it is the fourth of the fundamental needs that we have as human beings. To captivate your audience, help them make an enemy of the status quo and see the positive promise of tomorrow that is just out of reach and worth the effort. At some point in all of our lives, we wake up and stand before the insatiable chasm of existential meaninglessness. People want to make a difference. Give them the means and the will to make their dent in the universe.

Most of the time, the best way to approach topic selection is to pick a single unifying message that you want to deliver and then scour your brain for your amazing experiences that will add emotional depth to the logic of your message. If you get stuck, do it the other way around. No one will ever know. The key thing, and I cannot stress this enough, is that you need to have a crystal clear understanding of your central idea before you do anything else. One of the biggest mistakes that speakers make is trying to pack a lifetime worth of learning into a single talk. Laser focus on a single concept will give you a fine mesh filter for editing your material. If you have a great concept or story that does not directly support your message, then you have to omit it, no matter how much you want to use it.

Once you identify your single unifying message, you need to be able to communicate it in a way that your audience cannot forget. The next chapter will show you how to transform your central idea into a message that will attach itself to your listener's brains.

## Recap

- Inspire your audience with a single idea that either changes the way people think about their world or persuades them to take action.

- Create an audience-centric narrative layered with stories and facts.

- Connect with people's deep rooted needs for belonging, self interest, self-actualization, or hope in the future.

# CHAPTER 3

# HOW TO CRAFT YOUR CATCHPHRASE

A few years before he delivered his inspirational TED masterpiece, Simon Sinek had a revelation. He figured out the common thread that explains why some leaders and some companies succeed while others fail. Fortunately, he did not keep this to himself; after all, his life's purpose is to 'inspire others so that they can do the things that inspire them.' Simon's secret, which he shares freely with the world, is expressed by his Golden Circle concept. Simon builds a compelling case that average people and average companies start with what they do and, if you are lucky, share a little bit of how they do it. In contrast, inspiring leaders and remarkable companies first share why they do what they do, then share how they do what they do. They save what they do for last. Sinek's favorite example is Apple Inc. Apple's "why" is to empower individuals to challenge the status quo. Their "how" is by designing great physical and digital experiences at a cost that is affordable to the mainstream consumer. What Apple does is make computers and smart-phones in various sizes, shapes, and colors.

Simon's concept is not new; it was the foundation of the "mission statement" fad that was all the rage decades ago. He breathed new life into an old concept and inspired millions by communicating his message in a new way with fresh stories. Simon's first masterstroke was to encapsulate this concept in the elegant Golden Circle. It is admittedly clever, but it is not viral. Imagine that someone walks up to you and says "Hey, do you want the secret to success in business and life?" As you stand ready to absorb the wisdom of the ages, they add "It's simple dummy, it is The Golden Circle!" You are going to be pretty disappointed. Without further explanation, a golden circle has little meaning. It is not going to call you to action or change your perspective. But, Mr. Sinek had one more trick up his sleeve. He encapsulated his concept in an unforgettable catchphrase – "Start With Why". (This is also the name of his book.) Those three words tell you unambiguously what you need to do right now to change your life for the better.

Simon and his cohort of TED speakers make their ideas spreadable by turning their central idea into a foundational phrase, a power-bite, that they repeat until it becomes implanted in their audience's mind. Simon actually has a couple. In addition to "start with why", he has "people don't buy what you do, they buy why you do it" and "work with people who believe what you believe."

So, what makes a great catchphrase? First, keep it short. Three words are best but you can get away with up to twelve. Conjure up President Obama one more time since this is his go-to recipe for sticky message pudding: "Hope And Change", "Pass This Bill", "We Can't Wait", "Yes We Can". Get the gist?

The second defining characteristic of catchphrases is that they issue a clear call to action. "Start with why" is a great example of this. Johnny Cochran's "If it doesn't fit, you must acquit" has remained in the public consciousness for over 15 years. Cochran's jury instruction and Mr. Sinek's observation "people don't buy what you do..." share the third key characteristic of power-bites. They have a musical, often rhyming, quality that makes them catchy. To truly understand that particular nearly rhyming "quality" requires a brief grammar lesson (I promise to make it as painless as possible.) To make a phrase musical, you can repeat a word or phrase at the beginning (anaphora) or the end (epistrophe) of successive clauses. Dickens hammered his readers with anaphora at the beginning of the <u>Tale of Two Cities</u>:

*"It was the best of times, it was the worst of times, it was the age of wisdom, it was the age of foolishness, it was the epoch of belief, it was the epoch of incredulity, it was the season of Light, it was the season of Darkness, it was the spring of hope, it was the winter of despair, we had everything before us, we had nothing before us, we were all going direct to Heaven, we were all going direct the other way- in short, the period was so far like the present period, that some of its noisiest authorities insisted on its being received, for good or for evil, in the superlative degree of comparison only."*

So that you do not get too carried away, take note of the fact that most people can really only remember the first bit: "It was the best of times, it was the worst of times." That is the upper bound of the three to twelve words rule-of-thumb you encountered earlier. If you do want to get fancy, try symploce, which is the combination of anaphora and epistrophe. In plain language, symploce is repeating words or phrases at the beginning as well as repeating (generally different) words or phrases at the end of successive clauses.

Simon Sinek's "People don't buy what you do, they buy why you do it" uses a fourth weapon in this rhetorical arsenal.

He repeats the same word in different parts of the phrase. The grammar police call this traductio. If all that was too much, then just resort to the old standby and rhyme your catchphrase.

Alright, we covered catchphrase length, action orientation, and musical rhythm. There are two more quick characteristics that are important and interrelated. When you construct a two part catchphrase, make the second part positive and sharply contrasting with the first part. "People don't buy what you do ..." is a negative statement that triggers one's brain to ask "Well then, what do they buy?" "...they buy why you do it" satisfies the listener's immediate need to know.

The way you order these contrasting pairs matters. That is the last property of a viral catchphrase. Like a well designed joke, you need to put the punch word or punch phrase at the end. "You must acquit if the glove doesn't fit" simply does not have the same oomph.

With a compelling, laser-focused single unifying message packaged into a catchphrase that makes it viral, you will have entered the upper echelon of speakers. Next, we turn to building out your speech, including the way that you are introduced.

## Recap

- Make your idea viral by encapsulating it in an unforgettable catchphrase that is between three and twelve words.

- Craft your catchphrase to be action-oriented and rhythmic.

- Repeat your catchphrase at least three times during your presentation.

# CHAPTER 4

# HOW TO BE INTRODUCED

Unfortunately, TED videos do not show the manner in which speakers are introduced. There is also not much in the way of information on the "TED-way" for speaker introductions in the public domain. Though a bad introduction will probably not sink a great talk, a great introduction lasting no more than a minute or two can provide a powerful launching pad into your speech.

One of the most viewed TED speakers of all time is Hans Rosling, who manages to vibrantly bring life to otherwise dull reams of public health data. The core message in his talk is that we can join together to raise global health standards by freely sharing public health data and analytical tools. Let me start out by showing you what a terrible introduction to Hans' revolutionary talk might have sounded like:

*"Ladies and gentlemen. Today, it is my pleasure to introduce Dr. Hans Rosling, Professor of International Health at Karolinska Institute in Stockholm. In his early academic career, Dr. Rosling studied statistics and medicine ultimately becoming a licensed physician in 1976. As a result of his discovery and subsequent investigation of an outbreak of konzo, a paralytic disease, Hans earned his Ph.D. from Uppsala University in 1986. He has won over 10 prestigious awards, including The Gannon Award in 2010 for the continued pursuit of human advancement. In 2011 Dr. Rosling was ranked one of the 100 most creative people in business by Fast Company Magazine and was elected as a member of the Swedish Academy of Engineering Sciences. If his professional accomplishments do not impress you enough, he is also a renowned sword swallower. Please put your hands together and give a warm TED welcome to Dr. Hans Rosling!"* (Source: a completely fictitious introduction made up using Wikipedia information)

Blah blah blah blah. Just writing that nearly put me to sleep. In fact, I am going to keep a copy of that introduction on my night table as a cure for insomnia and I recommend you do the same. By contrast, great introductions are relevant to the speaker's core message, are audience centric, and establish the speaker's credibility without placing him or her on a pedestal. Consider each of these qualities in turn.

Constructive introductions are limited in scope to information that ties to the speaker's central unifying idea. Dr. Rosling took the stage to inspire the influential TED conference attendees to support the spread of free public health databases. That he earned his Ph.D. in 1986 from Uppsala University for discovering and investigating an outbreak of a rare disease is admirable and amazing but not directly relevant to the core message of the talk. A better, on point, piece of information is that Dr. Rosling was chairman of the Karolinska International Research and Training Committee where he started health research collaborations with universities in Asia, Africa, the Middle East, and Latin America. That factoid previews that the man about to take the stage has a passion for advancing public health through global partnerships.

A far more egregious flaw of the fake introduction above is that it fails to tell the audience what is in it for them. People do not sit in a chair for hours on end listening to other people speak unless they are going to get a return on their investment of time and attention. A great introduction tempts the audience with a taste of the benefit they are going to get but does not go so far as to give away the bacon.

A better introduction might have included something to the effect of "By the end of Hans' talk, you will learn the way that sharing global health data will enhance the quality of your life, the lives of your children, and the lives of seven billion of your closest friends." With that small change, the audience has a reason to sit up and pay attention.

Emcees must establish the speaker's credibility without making them appear superhuman. Though we respect authority, we trust people who are similar. We are inspired to alter our perspective and to rise to action by people just like us who started out as skeptics but succeeded after embracing change. The problem with the introduction above is that it paints Dr. Rosling as a genius among geniuses. He is a statistician, a medical doctor, an epidemiologist, and has garnered countless accolades. Any person that hears this introduction will say "Hans Rosling is amazing. But, I can never do what he has done because I do not have his pedigree and his IQ." In this case, it is enough to say the following: "Dr. Rosling is Professor of International Health at Karolinska Institute and an important contributor to advancing the global discussion on public health." This is enough to establish the speaker's credibility and again ties directly to what he is about to discuss. Finally, the sword swallowing bit humanizes the good doctor, but in a circus-freak sort of way that is also not relevant to the topic at hand.

Most of the time, the person who introduces you will not know you from Adam. In that case, you should provide a written introduction that follows the three tenets discussed above by sharing what is in it for the audience, by maximizing topical relevance, and by minimizing biographical information. Make sure to take the time to review the introduction with the emcee and even have him or her practice it once or twice to get the timing and delivery down. That last step is almost always skipped and sadly results in a bored audience.

On the other hand, something magical can happen when the emcee knows you even just a little; I know this firsthand. In 2011, I was invited to Portland to speak to a group of eighty members of the entrepreneur peer mentoring group StarveUps. My central theme was secrets to delivering presentations that help little companies close big company deals. Just before we took the stage, John Friess, a busy entrepreneur and the evening's emcee, admitted to me that he had neglected to review my introduction. He took a brief look at the copy I handed him, crumpled it up, put it in his pocket and said "Trust me." Needless to say, my blood pressure immediately rose more than a few points. John took the stage and proceeded to tell a brief personal story about his struggles with pitching to investors, partners, and customers. He then shared with the audience the story of how he met me and of my passion for trying to give everyone I meet the tools and the feedback they need to become inspiring communicators. I could not have asked for a better introduction.

The final consideration in crafting an introduction for your emcee is that the content should match the tone of your speech. I hope that the person who introduced Hans Rosling did not kick things off with a mini comedy routine. In contrast, a comic introduction is perfectly appropriate and highly desirable as a warm-up act for a funny speaker. The synchronization between the introduction and the speech helps manage the energy level in the room – something that will be discussed at length in the next chapter.

Once the emcee starts the applause and shakes your hand, it is time to open your speech. I'll cover great openings in the next chapter.

**Recap**

- Write a one to two minute introduction for your emcee that connects to your core message.

- Ensure that your introduction shares why you are the right person to share your idea with the audience.

- Craft an introduction that positions you as a credible guide not as a super-human.

# CHAPTER 5

# HOW TO OPEN YOUR TALK

In literature and poetry, structure is accepted as a liberating force for creativity, rather than a limiting constraint. This is evident in the five-seven-five rhythm of the haiku or the sonnet form, which both give rise to infinite beauty and variation. I feel that that same phenomenon holds true in the world of speech-craft. There is always an opening, a body, and a conclusion. The art is in how the speaker fills her canvas.

Of the countless ways to begin your speech, I am going to detail the three types of openings that the most compelling TED speakers use to engage their audiences. Remember that the first ten or twenty seconds of your speech is the peak of your audience's engagement level. It is not going to get any better as one by one your listeners will get distracted by their mental grocery lists or the next day's outfit. Hook them fast with benefits by giving them an implicit or explicit reason to pay close attention.

The most consistently successful opening is the personal story. Though we will go in to much greater depth on storytelling in an upcoming chapter, here is what you need to remember. First, your personal story should really be personal. Tell your own story and share your observations. It is a good idea to make others the heroes in your stories. Second, make sure your story is directly relevant to your core message. If your goal is to inspire people to volunteer their time to feed the homeless, a cute story about how your dog can bark 'I love you' just does not belong. Third, fourth, and fifth, make your story highly emotional, highly sensory, and rich in dialogue. The story should be so specific that your audience is able to relive it with you.

In his TEDTalk, author and success expert Richard St. John demonstrated the power of using a personal story for his opening:

*This is really a two hour presentation I give to high school students, cut down to three minutes. And it all started one day on a plane, on my way to TED, seven years ago. And in the seat next to me was a high school student, a teenager, and she came from a really poor family. And she wanted to make something of her life, and she asked me a simple little question. She said, "What leads to success?" And I felt really badly, because I couldn't give her a good answer. So I get off the plane, and I come to TED. And I think, jeez, I'm in the middle of a room of successful people! So why don't I ask them what helped them succeed, and pass it on to kids?*

Did you visualize yourself on the plane? Did you turn your head and eavesdrop when the teenage girl, who came from a poor family, asked Richard for the secret of success? Could you feel Richard's disappointment about not having a good answer and his zeal to be ready to help kids in the future? Moreover, and more selfishly, are you now intensely curious what Richard St. John found to be the key to success? To find out, you will have to watch his talk on TED.com; I cannot spoil all the fun. But, at least you now know Richard's secret to capturing his audience with a personal story opening.

Note that Richard St. John was giving a super-short TEDTalk, just three minutes compared to the TED maximum of eighteen minutes. If he had more time, then he could have added much more detail and dialogue. What was the girl's name? What did she look like? What was it like talking over the roar of the engines? How tantalizing was the aroma of freshly baked chocolate chip cookies wafting in from first class? How did this seemingly awkward conversation between an unaccompanied minor and businessman in his forties get started? You get the picture. Choose the right amount of detail for the time allotted just as Richard did.

In terms of effectiveness, the remaining two types of powerful openings pack an equally strong punch. In no particular order, let us address the shocking statement first. Though shocking statements most frequently rely on statistics, they can also express strong opinions that challenge conventional wisdom. The important thing is that your point must trigger a range of audience emotions. If you share a "what", then people will have a burning need to fill in the gaps on why, how, when, and where. In his TED2010 talk, celebrity chef and child nutrition advocate Jamie Oliver used exactly this recipe in his opening. Listen to how he started:

*Sadly, in the next eighteen minutes when I do our chat, four Americans that are alive will be dead from the food that they eat. My name is Jamie Oliver. I am thirty four years old. I am from Essex in England and for the last seven years I have worked fairly tirelessly to save lives in my own way. I am not a doctor; I'm a chef. I don't have expensive equipment, or medicine. I use information and education. I profoundly believe that the power of food has a primal place in our homes that binds us to the best bits of life.*

Chef Oliver captured his audience by sharing what is happening – people are dropping like flies from the food they eat. And, they are not half way around the world in a developing country; they are in the same modern nation as his audience. You should have little doubt that most of the audience is wondering if they will survive lunch! Such is the power of a shocking statistic that is deeply and personally relevant to the audience. Remember the magic four needs: physical health and safety; love and belonging; desire and self-interest; hope in a brighter future. Jamie went primal, life and death, and had his audience waiting with bated breath to find out why this is happening and to learn how to stay alive.

Asking a powerful question is the third reliable speech opening. In some ways, this is a variation of the shocking statement approach, but you are more explicit about what you want your audience to think about. For example, Jamie Oliver could have started out with "Why is it that 320 ordinary Americans just like you die every day from the food they eat?"

If you go the powerful question route, I recommend that you use "why" questions and "how" questions. "Why" questions are by far the most enticing since they tap into our natural curiosity to understand the world around us. Once we know why things happen, then we want to know how to make good things happen and how to prevent bad things from happening. If the "why" is implied or well understood, then you can open with a "how" question. Consider Mr. Oliver's message one more time. He could have led with: "How can you prevent the food you eat from killing you?"

In the reformulated "why" and "how" openings I constructed for Jamie Oliver's speech, you probably noticed that I snuck the word "you" in a few times. That magic word transforms a good question into a great question by putting your listeners in introspective mode. You want them thinking about themselves and their world.

Simon Sinek demonstrated the most effective use of a powerful question opening of any TEDTalk that I have encountered. Here is how he began a talk that ultimately provided people with a how-to framework for being an inspiring leader or an effective corporation:

*How do you explain when things don't go as we assume? Or better, how do you explain when others are able to achieve things that seem to defy all of the assumptions? For example: Why is Apple so innovative? Year after year, after year, after year, they're more innovative than all their competition. And yet, they're just a computer company. They're just like everyone else. They have the same access to the same talent, the same agencies, the same consultants, the same media. Then why is it that they seem to have something different? Why is it that Martin Luther King led the Civil Rights Movement? He wasn't the only man who suffered in a pre-civil rights America. And he certainly wasn't the only great orator of the day. Why him? And why is it that the Wright brothers were able to figure out control-powered, manned flight when there were certainly other teams who were better qualified, better funded, and they didn't achieve powered man flight, and the Wright brothers beat them to it. There's something else at play here.*

A single opening question is sufficient. But, Mr. Sinek instead chose to bombard his audience with a string of "why" questions. This approach, an extended "why-tease", is extremely effective but must be done carefully. To successfully string multiple questions together in an opening, they must all have the same answer. Simon even mixed how and why questions together, a bit like playing with matches and dynamite; however, both types of questions were rooted in the same underlying reason. I would just leave you confused if I opened a speech with "Why is it that the sky is blue? And why is it that that a rolling stone gathers no moss? And why is it that elephants are afraid of mice?"

We looked at the three most effective ways that TED speakers open their speeches. They use personal stories, shocking statements, or compelling questions. Now, let's kick it up a notch and look at pre-openings and post-openings. Say what?

Nine out of ten times, you will want to go right into your choice of one of the three standard opening styles. The other time you need to do something different, and it has everything to do with the level of energy in the room. World class speakers strive to mirror the energy in the room at the opening and then lead their audience on an emotional journey for the remainder of their talk. However, sometimes there is too much or too little tension in the room. That is when the speaker needs to pull out a pre-opening.

I presume that when Sir Ken Robinson delivered his TED Talk on education reform, the audience was restless after hours or days of sitting and listening. Even being relentlessly inspired can be pretty taxing. Consequently, he was facing an audience with too much tension. In this case, he used the following humorous pre-opening as a release valve. If you are delivering a funny speech, it is critically important to get a laugh in the first thirty seconds to prime the audience. It took Ken Robinson less than ten:

*Good morning. How are you? It's been great, hasn't it? I've been blown away by the whole thing. In fact, I'm leaving. (Laughter) There have been three themes, haven't there, running through the conference, which are relevant to what I want to talk about. One is the extraordinary evidence of human creativity in all of the presentations that we've had and in all of the people here. Just the variety of it and the range of it. The second is that it's put us in a place where we have no idea what's going to happen, in terms of the future. No idea how this may play out...*

Mr. Robinson not only used humor, but also employed another technique to connect with his audience called an opening call-back. Typically, you encounter a call-back when standup comics close their set by referring back to an earlier joke or theme that had the audience in stitches. The opening call back in a keynote speech provides connective tissue between your material and the material of previous speakers. If there were no prior speakers, your opening call back could be to prominent current events, to audience members you met just before taking the stage, or to conditions in the room. The opening call back should have an impromptu feel to it. Like Sir Ken Robinson's, it should be personalized for the audience, thus making them feel special, making them feel that the talk you are about to give was custom crafted just for them.

A pre-opening can also be used when there is too little tension in the room. That can happen if you are going to give a very serious talk and the audience does not know what is coming. Since this is rare, I have never seen it used in a TEDTalk – most speeches have a good title and description of which the audience is aware. However, I have seen it in a couple of other forums. Ed Tate, Toastmasters World Champion of Public Speaking in 2000, is a master of this technique. In one of Ed's speeches, he precedes a powerful personal story of his experiences as the target of racial hatred with a very long silence. In fact, he stands quiet and motionless for ten full seconds before screaming a racial expletive. If ten seconds does not sound like a lot, try it out in front of an audience; it is an eternity of silence and discomfort for you and for the audience. It is also the most amazing tension builder in a speaker's toolbox. Use it sparingly.

One more interesting pre-opening is to ask your audience to imagine themselves in a particular situation or environment. Before sharing a story about how he studied the way his newborn son acquired language, MIT researcher Deb Roy invited his TED2011 audience to imagine life inside of a novel social experiment:

*Imagine if you could record your life – everything you said, everything you did, available in a perfect memory store at your fingertips, so you could go back and find memorable moments and relive them, or sift through traces of time and discover patterns in your own life that previously had gone undiscovered. Well that's exactly the journey that my family began five and a half years ago.*

Your opening should have caused your audience to consider the benefits of your talk in an implicit way. The post-opening, which should always exist, provides an explicit promise of the benefits that your audience will get and how long it will take to get them. For the longest time, I followed one of the three standard openings with a statement such as: "In the next forty five minutes, I will share with you the three secrets to happiness." That is a pretty good statement of benefits. "I will share" is lot better than "I will tell". However, it does have a couple of problems. First and foremost, it is speaker-centric and not audience-centric. The statement reveals what I am going to do, not what you are going to get. Second, it is not particularly sensory. A great post-opening should provide the audience with a visual metaphor of the structure of your speech. Applying these lessons, I would use the following: "Forty five minutes from now, you will walk out of here with the three A's of happiness in your toolbox." That statement is audience centric, it queues them to listen to my speech to pluck out the three A's, and has given them an action-oriented visual.

Catchy mnemonics, such as acronyms or frameworks like the "three A's", are a great way to provide a roadmap to your listeners. Resist the temptation to share what the acronym stands for at the beginning of your talk. The pleasure for the audience is in the progressive reveal over the course of your speech.

I have a strong preference for three's since that is the stickiest number. You can have three steps, three themes, three strategies, three tips, three techniques, three tools. If you doubt this rule-of-thumb, consider the following. Everyone knows, thanks to Stephen Covey, there are seven habits of highly effective people. Can you name them? There are Ten

Commandments and ten amendments to the United States Constitution that comprise the Bill of Rights. Jack Welch preached the four "E's" of leadership? Can you name them all? Thought so.

Since there is limitless variety to the way you open your speech, you should know at least a few bad openings so that you do not commit the same sins as your forbearers. Of course, TED is selective about which videos they share on TED.com. But, you may not be aware that they edit even the chosen videos to remove verbal slips and anything that is awkward, insulting or offensive. Consequently, it is impossible to find a terrible TED opening.

Nevertheless, there is plenty of badness out there from which to learn, so here is a quick list. Do not open with a quote – it is cliché even if it is relevant. Do not open with a joke, for the same reason. Do not open with anything even mildly offensive to your audience. Do not open with a Dilbert cartoon – oh, if I had a penny for that one... Do not open with "Thank you..." - if you want to thank your audience, do it at the end. Do not open with "Before I begin..." - since you just began.

There is one more type of opening that is almost always a bad idea. That is the activity opening. On the Internet, there is a fantastic speech posted to a video sharing site on the topic of charismatic leadership. The content is highly valuable and the presenter's delivery skills are impeccable. However, I took strong exception to his opening. To kick off his presentation, he asks his audience to stand up, put their hand on their heart, turn around, and take one step forward. He then goes on to say that he can now report back to his own boss when asked how the presentation went, that he 'got them on their feet, touched their heart, turned them around, and got them moving in the right direction.' It is a clever gimmick. But, if you look closely at the audience members, many are displaying the body language of people who just realized they have just been manipulated. Moreover, this trick had little or nothing to do with the speaker's core theme. In fact, in many ways, it actually negated the message of authentic leadership charisma.

Every rule has its exceptions and this is the case with avoiding activity openings too. If you have a very relevant activity that engages the audience and is fully genuine, then it can work. By way of example, in her TEDxFiDiWomen talk, Regena Thomashauer has the core objective of inspiring women to embrace pleasure as a doorway to power, passion, enthusiasm, and creativity. Mama Gena is carried onto the stage by three men with the sound of Pitbull's "I Know You Want Me" pulsing from the speakers. When the men set her down, she begins dancing and screams "Come on, dance with me!!!". As the camera pans back, you see that every person in the audience is instantly on their feet grooving to the beat. As the music dies down, she says:

*"Wasn't that fun? Did you love that? Do you know what I was doing? I was flooding your body with nitric oxide! Do you know why? Because whenever we have a pleasurable experience, there are huge physical consequences. With just thirty seconds of fun, your blood starts to oxygenate and circulate. Nitric oxide is released and that turns on these neurotransmitters including beta-endorphin and prolactin."*

In this instance, there was one hundred percent relevance between the activity – dancing – and the message. Mama Gena screams her passion and her purpose.

Once you finish your opening, you need to smoothly transition into the body of your speech.

**Recap**

- Start with a pre-opening if there is a mismatch between the tension in the audience and the tone of your speech.

- Open either with a personal story, a shocking statement, or a powerful question.

- Deliver a post-opening that provides an explicit promise of the benefits that your audience will get and how long it will take to get them

# CHAPTER 6

# HOW TO BUILD YOUR SPEECH BODY AND TRANSITIONS

Imagine that you are going to construct a building. You must first learn to lay a proper foundation and to apply the rules that govern supporting the walls and the roof. Your first building might be a bit sloppy with clumsily exposed structural support columns. But, you can rest assured that the building is going to stay standing. As you get more experienced, you learn to let form follow function. You learn to hide the structural elements when you want to hide them and expose them when you want them to stand out. Sometimes you follow the exposed "skin and bones" style of early Chicago skyscraper designer Ludwig Mies van der Rohe. Other times you apply the flowing, 'deconstructivist' style of Guggenheim Bilbao architect Frank Gehry.

The journey of the speaker is much like the journey of the modern architect. One of the first things that beginning speakers learn about organization is building a foundation using the framework: tell the audience what you are going to tell them, tell them, then tell them what you told them. That one great piece of advice is what makes speeches stand on their own without collapsing. Novice speakers interpret this advice quite literally. They will give a speech that goes something like this:

*Opening: Why is it that some fruits heal your body and others make you fat? Ten minutes from now, you will walk out of this room with a grocery list of super-fruits that are proven to add extra years to your life. The three fruits are acai berries, goji berries, and pomegranates.*

*Body: Let's explore the health benefits of the first super-fruit, acai berries...*

Compared to speeches that lack structure, this is a very solid start. The audience knows exactly where the speaker is going and they are primed to be convinced why these three fruits can really deliver a better and longer life. The problem, of course, is that the structural guts of the speech are too exposed. The key to advancing to the next level of speaking is to add the transition tease into your repertoire.

Consider the transition in the super-fruit speech example above. The imaginary speaker gave too much away by sharing the three super-fruits right off the bat. A better approach is to make a statement or to ask a question that gets the audience thinking about themselves while making them hungry for more. For example: "What if you knew the three super-fruits that could give you ten more years of active, healthy life? What if you knew that they are easy to find and easy to add to your breakfast, lunch, or dinner?" This question still primes the audience to listen for three items to add to their grocery list. It also teases them to remain interested as each super-fruit is revealed. Lastly, it opens the door for you to prove that the fruits really have the ability to keep people on the planet a little bit longer.

The body of your speech is your opportunity to deliver the "tell them" part of the framework. In most cases, your opening will share the "what'"; the body must then deliver the "why" and the "how". I strongly recommend that you build the body of your speech with three sections regardless of the length of your speech. If you have eighteen minutes, you need to provide more detail in each of the three sections than if you only have six minutes. Having no more and no less than three pieces will help you remember where you are going and will help your audience remember your message.

Though it does not really matter what narrative structure you choose for your talk, it is incredibly important that you choose one. The three most effective are the situation-complication-resolution framework, the chronological narrative, and the idea-concepts description.

The situation-complication-resolution structure offers the most efficient way to lead people on a three part journey that changes their perspective or calls them to action. In the first part, you describe the situation at hand in a fairly neutral way. A good way to do this is to imagine that you are providing background context to a person who is intelligent and interested, but does not have significant prior knowledge. In the second part, the complication section, you hook the audience by revealing why the current state of the world is flawed. Flaws not only may be problems but also may be hidden opportunities. In the final part, you offer the solution that neatly and completely resolves the problems or harnesses the opportunities you cited earlier.

In his TEDGlobal 2009 talk, Daniel Pink used the situation-complication-resolution framework to spread his idea about increasing the productivity and happiness of knowledge workers. The skeleton of his argument went like this: (Situation) For most of recorded history, management relied on extrinsic if-then rewards to motivate workers. This worked well for mechanical tasks. (Complication) By contrast, knowledge workers are highly motivated by intrinsic rewards. In fact, extrinsic rewards like monetary incentives actually reduce productivity for thinking tasks. (Resolution) Future leaders must install a new operating system for motivating workers that centers upon autonomy, mastery, and purpose.

The chronological narrative is a second, highly effective way to organize the flow of your TEDTalk. Some speakers reach back into history, as Eat, Pray, Love author Elizabeth Gilbert did in her TED2009 talk. In urging her audience to reject their fear and "keep showing up", Ms. Gilbert stepped through a timeline of human attitudes toward creativity spanning from Ancient Rome to the Renaissance to modern times. More commonly, speakers cast the spotlight on formative experiences in their own lives that relate to their central idea. Nigerian author Chimananda Adichie followed this approach in describing her own journey of understanding and ultimately embracing cultural diversity. She took us from her youth reading classical Western literature, to discovering African authors, to her American university experiences, and finally on a trip to Mexico.

Shorter TEDTalks tend to rely on the idea-concepts format. Think of this as the David Letterman top ten list style of presenting. This structure offers a very efficient way to enumerate best practices, facts, or arguments when there is not enough time to tell a complete story. Often the sequence of the concepts is interchangeable. For example, Richard St. John shared eight secrets of success including: (1) do it for love; (2) work hard; (3) practice and focus; (4) push through self-doubt and failure; (5) serve others something of value; (6) listen and observe to generate great ideas. (You will have to watch his talk to get the other two.)

Regardless of the narrative structure chosen, the best TED speeches treat each section as a bundle of "right brain" and "left brain" stimulation. Stories or activities pique the emotional right brain. Facts, strategies, tips, and techniques convince the left brain. You need either to persuade people to change their perception or to incite them to action. As your speech progresses, you are taking your audience on a primarily emotional journey. The facts allow you to anticipate, state, and acknowledge the logical objections that arise in naturally curious and instinctively skeptical human brains.

Imagine that you have a child with a life threatening peanut allergy. Moreover, imagine that you are speaking to an audience of fellow parents at your child's preschool with the objective of convincing them not to send their children to school with peanut butter and jelly sandwiches. If you took a facts-only approach you might say something like: "Did you know that 0.5% of all Americans have a life-threatening peanut allergy? That means that for 15 million of us, a peanut butter and jelly sandwich is as dangerous as a loaded gun." The audience members that have close friends and family with such allergies can be convinced with this approach. Others will listen with sympathy and interest before going to home to pack their kid's lunchbox with a PB&J.

To have real impact, you must couple your rational facts with emotional stories. For me, this example is all too real. Given the chance, I would add the following story to the statistics above.

*"On a hot August day in 2002, my wife and in-laws took my two year old daughter, Emma, to a fun outing of splashing and building sand castles on the Jersey shore. On their way back, they stopped at a bakery and gave her a bite of a peanut butter tart. During the car ride home, one hive turned into two and two into thousands as every inch of her tiny body swelled and reddened. When my family pulled into the driveway, I bounded blithely out of the front door, unaware of the situation, to see my little girl. My in-laws suggested we put Emma in the bath. I took one look at her and drove ninety miles per hour to the nearest emergency room. While we sat waiting to be admitted, she whispered the words 'Daddy, I love you' just before losing consciousness. I bolted out of my chair, holding her limp body in my*

*arms, and screamed 'Somebody, anybody help me!" Fortunately, a doctor came immediately with a life saving injection of adrenaline."*

While that story may not sway everyone, it is far more powerful than sharing facts alone.

During the course of each section, you should frequently ask questions to get the audience to reflect on their own lives. In smaller forums, you can actually solicit verbal responses. With larger audiences, you still want to ask questions. This is the way to transform a speech into a conversation. Audience members are still able to reply in their minds and with their body language.

Remember to interpret any statistics, particularly large numbers, with vivid, emotional, personally relevant analogies or metaphors. There is a huge difference between saying that "70 million Americans live every day with heart disease" and saying "Look at the three people closest to you. Odds are that one of the four of you has heart disease and that it will kill you." Similarly, Jamie Oliver's opening in the previous chapter skillfully revealed that four Americans would be dead from the food they eat by the time he finished his eighteen minute speech.

At the beginning of this chapter, you learned how to smoothly transition your speech from the opening into the first section of the body of your speech. To recap, one key to a smooth transition is employing a tease that holds the audience's interest. Openings are short enough that the transition tease is usually sufficient. However, when moving from one section of your speech body to the next, you need to do a little more. Speech body sections are typically longer in duration. In an eighteen minute TED speech, perhaps as long as five minutes. In that case, you need to summarize the section with call backs to the story you used or to the facts you revealed. Nigerian novelist Chimamanda Adichie did this to perfection in her TEDGlobal 2009 talk:

*Because all I had read were books in which characters were foreign, I had become convinced that books, by their very nature, had to have foreigners in them, and had to be about things with which I could not personally identify. (Pause) Now, things changed when I discovered African books. There weren't many of them available. And they weren't quite as easy to find as the foreign books.*

In this transition, she recalls with a broad brush the stories and the facts that she had just shared about her experiences growing up reading British books. She preceded her transitional phrase "Now things changed..." with a pause. She delivered the transition in a more subdued conversational tone as compared to the more passionate tone used in the main body sections. Adichie's transition was subtle and smooth, while clearly signaling to the audience that she was going to show how African literature contrasted with that of British and American literature.

**Recap**

- Construct transitions that reinforce the key message of the preceding section and tease your audience with benefits to be gleaned the next section.

- Build the three part body of your speech using the situation-complication-resolution narrative flow.

- Couple rational facts with emotional stories.

# CHAPTER 7

# HOW TO CONCLUDE YOUR TALK

Now, it is time to draft your conclusion. When you provide a clear signal that you are moving to the end of your speech, people will increase their level of attention. Thus, the language you use is critical. You can certainly get away with saying "And, in conclusion…" However, you can do better. For example, you could use "And so we come to the end of our journey today and to the beginning of your future…" or "Now it is time for you to make a decision…"

The conclusion is your final opportunity to inspire your audience to change their perspective or to call them to action. You must create a sense of urgency. One way to do that is to shorten your sentences and add passion to your voice. In addition, every aspect of your speech conclusion must tie to your central unifying theme. Your goal should be to reinforce the benefit to your audience, the "why", in your conclusion. Since change is hard, give your audience an easy next step they can take today to get moving in the right direction. If needed, you might want to pull out the fear card by including "The consequences of failure are..."

You built a case for change in your speech. Place yourself in your audience's shoes and ask yourself what final objections people may have. As a speaker, it may be hard to do this, so you may wish to engage a friend to play devil's advocate. You must address these final doubts.

Never conclude your TEDTalk with a bland, book report style summary. Additionally, resist all temptation to introduce new material at the end. TED speakers close their talks in a variety of ways. Among the most common is a call back to a personal story, shocking statistic, or provocative question with which they opened. Another option is a story of hope, typically about someone else that applied the "how" you provided in the body of the speech. Be careful not to make the concluding story center exclusively on you since that will put you on a pedestal and break your personal connection with the audience.

You can also explicitly issue an immediate call to action or a powerful question. Alternatively, say the first part of your catchphrase and have the audience say the last part. For example, Simon Sinek could have ended by saying "People don't buy what you do, they buy..." and then paused to let the audience finish his sentence with "... why you do it."

Brene Brown, a professor at the University of Houston College of Social Work, delivered one of the most powerful speech conclusions I have ever heard in a TEDTalk. Dr. Brown's goal was to have people change their perspective on vulnerability from a source of pain to a source of power. She taught her audience to embrace vulnerability in order to live a fulfilled and a fulfilling life. She reinforced the message in the following conclusion:

*But there's another way, and I leave you with this. This is what I have found: to let ourselves be seen, deeply seen, vulnerably seen; to love with our whole hearts, even though there's no guarantee – and that's really hard, and I can tell you as a parent, that's excruciatingly difficult – to practice gratitude and joy in those moments of terror, when we're wondering, "Can I love you this much? Can I believe in this this passionately? Can I be this fierce about this?" just to be able to stop and, instead of catastrophizing what might happen, to say, "I'm just so grateful, because to feel this vulnerable means I'm alive." And the last, which I think is probably the most important, is to believe that we're enough. Because when we work from a place I believe that says, "I'm enough," then we stop screaming and start listening, we're kinder and gentler to the people around us, and we're kinder and gentler to ourselves.*

*That's all I have. Thank you.*

Notice that Brene Brown used not one but three transitional phrases to signal that she was moving into her conclusion: "But there is another way", "I leave you with this", and "This is what I have found." Each of these phrases was separated by an attention grabbing pause. Her conclusion is powerful, personal, and emotional. Her questions raise the tension level of the audience by touching the electric rail of self-doubt. Then, she immediately provides a salve of inspiring affirmations. "I'm enough." The enemy of good is great, so I am a bit wary to mess with the near perfection of Brene's speech. However, if I could make one change it would be to replace the "I" and "we" centric language with the singular "you."

One final thought on closing out your speech. An eternal debate rages as to whether or not the last words out of your mouth should be "thank you." In the yes camp, supporters say it is a final act of gratitude to cement your bond with the audience. In the no camp, detractors retort that it steals from your central message and may expose a little crack in your armor of confidence. They are both right and there really is no correct answer. What I can say is that almost every TED speaker ends their speech with "thank you" so you may wish to also follow this unwritten rule. A good alternative is the way that Nigel Marsh ended his talk on achieving work life balance: "And that, I think, is an idea worth spreading."

Throughout your talk, you should have been blending stories and facts. The stories really are the centerpiece since the desire to change is emotional not logical. In the next chapter, we will see how TED speakers craft compelling stories.

## Recap

- Employ language that clearly signals you are concluding your talk.

- Share the "why" that powers your single unifying idea.

- Call the audience to action with an easy next step and a sense of urgency.

# CHAPTER 8

# HOW TO TELL STORIES

If you would like to bore people to tears until they tear out their hair and claw their eyes out, then hammer them with facts for the entire eighteen minutes of your TEDTalk. Of course, the TED organizers will never let you get away with that. Every part of your speech, the opening, the body, and the conclusion, offers an opportunity to tell a story. You may choose to tell a single drawn out story as Jill Bolte Taylor did when she described studying her own stroke. Or you may wish to tell a sequence of stories as many equally excellent TED speakers have done.

The first question that arises is which story or stories should you tell? The easy answer is that it is always best to tell stories drawn from your personal experience or observation. Do you have to? No. A good exception to the rule is to bring stories of academic research to life. Malcolm Gladwell, author of <u>Blink</u> and <u>Tipping Point</u> and all around chronicler of pop psychology, did this in his famous "spaghetti sauce" speech. The central message of the speech is that embracing the diversity of human beings is the surest way to happiness. People do not want spaghetti sauce, they want spaghetti sauces. To prove the point, Mr. Gladwell needed to tell a story about someone else.

*So I decided instead, I would talk about someone who I think has done as much to make Americans happy as perhaps anyone over the last 20 years, a man who is a great personal hero of mine: someone by the name of Howard Moskowitz, who is most famous for reinventing spaghetti sauce.*

*Howard's about this high, and he's round, and he's in his 60s, and he has big huge glasses and thinning grey hair, and he has a kind of wonderful exuberance and vitality, and he has a parrot, and he loves the opera, and he's a great aficionado of medieval history.*

In those few sentences, Mr. Gladwell did two brilliant but subtle things. First, he brought the graying, quirky Howard Moskowitz visually to life. He did this by following the "show, don't tell" rule of storytelling. Malcolm could have said 'Dr. Moskowitz is a well rounded renaissance man.' That would be telling. Instead, he accomplished that same goal in a more effective way by showing us Howard's interest in parrots, opera, and medieval history. He made the description highly sensory.

Malcolm Gladwell's second clever choice was to make Howard Moskowitz the hero. As a speaker, one of the worst things you can do is put yourself on a pedestal. Position yourself as an equal, perhaps a guide, but not superior to your listeners. Making someone else the hero in your personal stories or in the stories of others you choose to tell is a great way to do that. That allows you to become human by sharing your failures, your flaws, and your frustrations. One of my favorite speaking experts is Craig Valentine, the 1999 Toastmasters World Champion of Public Speaking, who says that you should "come across as similar (*to your audience*) but with a special process." The special process is the 'how' that you are selflessly sharing.

Eat, Pray, Love author Elizabeth Gilbert unintentionally violated this rule in her TED2009 talk by mentioning her sudden success:

*And the peculiar thing is that I recently wrote this book, this memoir called "Eat, Pray, Love" which, decidedly unlike any of my previous books, went out in the world for some reason, and became this big, mega-sensation, international bestseller thing.*

Though she was very innocently using this as a set up for a self-deprecating joke about how she could never top this feat again, the damage was done. She actually does it again just before the end of her speech when she refers to her forthcoming book as "the dangerously, frighteningly over-anticipated follow up to my freakish success." Ms. Gilbert meant well, she really did. She was honestly surprised by her success; perhaps the most surprised person on the planet. The problem is that sharing your astonishment at your own success puts you on a pedestal. This transgression was clearly not the end of the world for Gilbert, as her talk on overcoming self-doubt and following your passion is the eleventh most viewed TEDTalk of all time; it positively affected millions of lives including my own. However, avoid self-aggrandizement, or even the appearance of it.

Once you have chosen the general type of story to tell, you have to structure the plot. You will never go wrong with the tried and true approach of starting with characters, putting them in emotion-provoking conflict, and then providing a conclusion. This is the classic hero's journey or quest.

Authentic characters, with all of their warts and complexity, are the basis for any riveting story. By identifying with specific character traits, listeners imagine themselves or people they care about as the protagonists. To help your audience form this bond, introduce your characters at the beginning of your story with highly descriptive language. Though human beings are the most effective characters for this purpose, you can easily substitute companies, animals, settings, or whatever suits your purpose. In order to set the stage for the coming conflict, make sure to clearly communicate the needs and desires of your characters.

Invite the audience into your story to relive it with you by re-enacting characters and their reactions. Each character should have a distinct personality. This includes: what is seen including posture and gestures; what is heard, the tone of their voice; what is implied such as their traits and desires. Instead of narrating what the characters do, give them dynamic, conversational dialogue. It is alright to embellish to a degree.

Note that your characters should also have fixed locations on the stage. When you embody a particular character, go stand in his or her spot on the stage. When you need to narrate, a nice technique is to step forward toward the audience and then step back into character.

By putting obstacles between your characters and their needs, you inject conflict in a way that triggers your audience's sense of empathy and their desire to problem solve. Presenting even a single obstacle can be highly effective when you have limited time to convey a story. However, your best strategy is to build progressively more intense barriers for your characters to overcome, all the while keeping the carrot just in front of their noses. This will fuel intensity and suspense. The barriers you erect can involve intrapersonal, interpersonal, or societal conflict.

At the climax of your story, follow a best practice of Hollywood screenwriters. A choice between good and evil is easy and uninteresting. Credible characters always take the minimum conservative action at every step in their journey. Compelling stories force the hero to choose between two goods, or more commonly, between two evils.

Every story should have a complete positive or negative ending. (Yes, a cliffhanger is the third option, but that is best saved for movies with planned sequels.) Stories with positive endings are highly effective for inspiration. They make people believe, 'I can do that.' In contrast, cautionary tales are more effective for teaching. Since pleasure is a more powerful long term motivation than pain, I recommend telling stories with positive endings the vast majority of the time. Your story conclusion is your opportunity to transfer wisdom. By ending with the way the story you described made you feel, you add additional depth through emotional disclosure.

The time to pull out the calamity tale is when you are trying to instill the virtues of safety to audiences that work in dangerous professions like construction or law enforcement. Nothing says "pay attention" more than 'listen up, or you might be the next one to die in a careless, preventable accident.' If you do tell a story that ends in disaster, spend time at the end exploring ways that the characters could have avoided their fate.

The mark of a great story is that it allows the listener to discover layer upon layer of wisdom through interpretation. This subtlety lies in not being overtly outcome focused. To enable the listener to peel the onion, you must make your stories rich in personal, emotional content as well as vivid sensory detail.

Stories need not be objective. In fact, the most compelling stories are told from a subjective point of view. You need your emotions to shine through and that can only be achieved if you express your most strongly held beliefs. An interesting twist on this theme is to tell a story sequentially from multiple, distinct points of view.

Above all, you will be far more successful with upbeat stories than with negative ones, even in an environment of disillusionment; if applicable, first acknowledge what is wrong, and then move toward positive outcomes. People crave speakers and stories that are authentic, yes, but also passionate and fun.

You may actually wish to draw out the emotional arc of your story. This arc is the escalating progression that gets your characters from their current state to their desired state.

Figure 8.1: Sample story arc (also your audience's emotional journey)

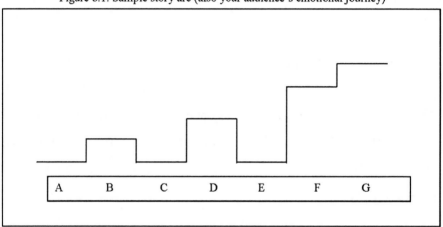

In the figure above, characters begin their journey stuck at point A, the current state, with their future at stake. By analogy, your audience begins their journey at point A with healthy skepticism or downright disbelief. At point B, the protagonist encounters her first obstacle and reacts in a way that moves her positively forward. However, at point C, the hero discovers that the action taken was necessary but not sufficient. Then, she encounters and reacts to overcome another challenge at point D. Again, the tension resumes when the protagonist discovers at point E that the second action was also necessary, but still not sufficient. Point F involves the third and most intense hurdle. Only by combining the three actions can the hero reach her desired state at point G and achieve a new normal. The entire arc encompasses either three actions to take or three strategies to apply.

In your talk, every key point should be delivered with a powerful one-two punch of story and fact. The techniques outlined in this chapter will help you weave an emotionally powerful, dialogue rich narrative. In the next part of the book, you will learn how to apply the verbal and non-verbal delivery skills of TED's master storytellers.

## Recap

- Tell stories drawn from your personal experience or observation.

- "Show, don't tell" using highly sensory description, authentic characters, and rich dialogue.

- Take your audience on an emotional journey as your characters encounter and overcome obstacles on an ultimately successful quest.

# PART-II

# DELIVERY & DESIGN

# CHAPTER 9

# HOW TO MASTER YOUR VERBAL DELIVERY

To properly grace the TED stage, you must master your verbal delivery. Fortunately, you have fertile opportunities to practice, as public speaking should be an amplified version of everyday conversation. This is of course a double edged sword. The imperfections that exist in your regular speech will be magnified during presentations. However, with a small amount of practice you can transform your verbal delivery both on and off stage.

With the exception of spoken word artists and classically trained storytellers, TED speakers tend to adopt one of two speaking personas. If you are an academic, then you can take on the nutty professor persona. You know this style when you see it since your brain screams 'Wow, that person is a super nerd and proud of it!'

Most TED presenters adopt the tone of a passionate one-on-one conversationalist. To pull this off, speak in your own voice with authenticity, interest, and humility. Use clear, everyday, jargon-free language packaged into short, complete sentences. The average TED Talk employs language at a sixth grade level. Your own enthusiastic interest should shine through with infectious curiosity, wonder, and awe. To demonstrate humility, assume the role of a guide who freely shares expertise, not ego. Even the whiff of self-promotion will turn off your audience.

Steve Jobs exemplified the passionate conversationalist. You can see glimpses of this in his touching Stamford University commencement address in 2005, but it is even more evident in his MacWorld addresses in later years. His language is filled with superlatives such as "amazing" and "incredible." Listening to him, you believed he was trying to challenge the status quo to make the world a better place and you wanted to join his crusade.

If you are like most people, then your speech has become infected with filler words. People use filler words because they are uncomfortable with silence. The most common are "um" and "ah", but the more evolved have masked these with "so", "actually" and even the occasional lip smack. More insidious, though in the same category, are the words and phrases "like", "you know", "sort of" and "kind of" since they express uncertainty, not to mention immaturity, in what you are saying.

The most potent cure for the filler word plague is the "burst and pause" method. Speak in bursts punctuated by pauses. The pause not only replaces filler words, but also gives you an aura of self-control. A brief silence provides time to collect and structure your next burst of thoughts. Beyond the personal benefits, the pause gives your audience the time they need to process what you are saying. Longer pauses add dramatic emphasis like a subtle yet powerful exclamation point. They grab your audience's attention. The pause is a gift that keeps on giving.

One you have eliminated most filler words by mastering the art of the pause, you must add vocal variety to make your speech interesting. Start by modulating your volume. If you speak softer, you will actually cause people to lean forward in their seats and take notice. If louder, then you command attention. Either way, take full, deep breaths and project so that people in the last row can hear you. Next, vary the speed. For example, you can gradually increase the speed and shorten sentences to add excitement. To add even more drama, vary pitch (high and low) and cadence (rhythmic rise and fall of voice inflection).

Your verbal delivery extends beyond speech mechanics into the words that you use. To enhance your audience's interest, you should make liberal use of vivid, descriptive, sensory detail. Sights, sounds, and smells are the easiest to incorporate. In some situations, you may even be able to weave in taste and touch. The small penalty you pay in being verbose is more than made up for by the impact you have of allowing your audience to form a mental picture.

In his 1936 classic "How To Win Friends and Influence People", Dale Carnegie said "Remember that a person's name is to that person the sweetest and most important sound in any language." When speaking to ten or more people let alone hundreds or thousands, it is not practical to address people by name. However, you can get very close by consistently using "you" in the singular. In fact, the best TED speakers use the word you twice as much as they use the word I.

Beware of using forms of "you" in the plural such as the phrases "you all", "everyone", "all of you", or "some of you". The same thing applies to words that envelop you and your entire audience such as "we" and "us". Instead of asking "How many of you have…", ask "Have you…" or "Raise your hand if you have…"

**Recap**

- Adopt the tone of a passionate one-on-one conversationalist.

- Add vocal variety by modulating your volume and pace.

- Make liberal use the word "you" in the singular.

# CHAPTER 10

# HOW TO ADD HUMOR TO YOUR TALK

I am not naturally funny. At least I do not think I am. But, sometimes we all want to tap into our inner Jerry Seinfeld. This chapter will give you a few simple techniques to bring humor to your presentations.

The fundamental principle to remember is that humor is rooted in surprise. As human beings, we delight in a twist that challenges our expectations and our sensibilities. That is why you find the punch-line or punch-word at the end. For example, consider the following joke attributed to Joe Pasquale: "See this, it's my step ladder. My real one left when I was three." Or better still, at least if you are a math nerd or know one, reflect upon this joke of unknown origin: "An independent variable is one that does not need other variables to feel good about itself." In both of these examples, the humor comes from the unexpected twist at the end that challenges what your brain was expecting.

Self-deprecating humor is easy and effective. As a society, we are conditioned to keep up appearances. So, we laugh with automatic delight when speakers let their guard down and reveal that they are in fact human. We laugh when others reveal their bad judgment. We laugh when they share their character flaws. We even laugh when people share stories of their physical pain – as long as they managed to survive. Although, come to think of it, Mel Brooks took it one step further: "[From your perspective] tragedy is when you break a nail, comedy is when I fall through an open manhole and die."

In her 2008 TEDTalk, brain researcher Jill Bolte Taylor described how she studied her own stroke as it happened. This topic could bring people to tears. And yet, Ms. Taylor had her audience rolling on the floor laughing by revealing to them what a super-nerd she is:

*"And in that moment, my right arm went totally paralyzed by my side. Then I realized, 'Oh my gosh! I'm having a stroke! I'm having a stroke!' And the next thing my brain says to me is, 'Wow! This is so cool. This is so cool!' How many brain scientists have the opportunity to study their own brain from the inside out?"*

Exaggerated reality is always good for a laugh. The simple way to express humor through exaggerated reality is to put a normal person in an extraordinary situation or an extraordinary person in a normal situation. Some examples of this are nonchalantly ignoring extreme danger, reacting excessively to minor offenses, and relentlessly pursuing futility.

Sir Ken Robinson, the most viewed TED speaker to date, puts an extraordinary person – Shakespeare – in an ordinary situation:

*"Because you don't think of Shakespeare being a child, do you? Shakespeare being seven? I never thought of it. I mean, he was seven at some point. He was in somebody's English class, wasn't he? How annoying would that be? 'Must try harder.' Being sent to bed by his dad, you know, to Shakespeare, 'Go to bed, now,' to William Shakespeare, 'and put the pencil down. And stop speaking like that. It's confusing everybody.'"*

We love to bring down authority a few notches. Experts who study why we laugh have determined that instance is when we, as listeners, feel a sense of superiority. This of course can result in some very cruel and offensive humor of which you should steer clear in your TEDTalk, not to mention in your life. However, there are some constituencies that are still politically correct to make fun of, such as academics and politicians.

Social scientist Hans Rosling, in his 2007 TEDTalk on global economic development takes aim at the academic elite:

*"But one late night, when I was compiling the report, I really realized my discovery. I have shown that Swedish top students know statistically significantly less about the world than the chimpanzees (sic)... I did also an unethical study of the professors of the Karolinska Institute – that hands out the Nobel Prize in Medicine, and they are on par with the chimpanzee."*

Embed humor in your dialogue-rich stories. Rather than describe how she was feeling, Jill Bolte Taylor in the example above expertly incorporates humor in internal dialogue. Similarly, Sir Ken Robinson places the humor in the words of Shakespeare's English teacher and Shakespeare's father.

Learn to 'riff.' You are likely to ask the question: "How funny do I need to be in a keynote?" To answer that question, consider the extremes. Professional standup comics deliver four to five jokes per minute. That is too much for a keynote, and actually quite superhuman. In contrast, Bill Gates delivered one joke every ten minutes in a TEDTalk that felt a bit flat.

In my moderately scientific analysis, the most viewed TED speakers deliver an average of one joke per minute in their keynote speeches. The best deliver around two jokes per minute. The secret is that the jokes are not evenly spread out. When they hit a funny theme, they 'riff' on the theme with clusters of three, progressively funnier quips. Sir Ken Robinson is the master of this.

As speakers, we sometimes forget that we have more than just words at our disposal. Especially with humor, there are several non-verbal techniques that you can use to amplify the laughs you get. The simplest adjustments are to synchronize your facial expressions and your gestures with your humor. Jim Carey is the greatest contemporary comic genius in the use of facial expressions. However, you do not need to go that far in your presentations. Even more subtle queues like wide, flashbulb eyes combined with raised eyebrows give your audience the signal to laugh. Since your humor will likely be embedded in stories, show your facial reactions in response to other character's dialogue. Physicality and movement can have the same amplifying effect. For example, you can make a character appear nervous or skittish though frenetic movement.

Outside of being offensive, there is only one other major aspect of humor to avoid in your public speaking. At all costs, avoid telling jokes that you heard or read somewhere else. This type of joke is often referred to as a public domain joke or a street joke. People that have heard a joke before will dismiss you as unoriginal. Those who have not heard the joke will instantly sense that it is canned. The ancient art of telling one-liners is obsolete; standup comics must now concentrate on exaggerating social commentary and personal experience. Create original humor by dramatizing the characters, stories, and dialogue in your personal stories.

Public speaking can be nerve wracking and trying to tell jokes often heightens your anxiety level. But, you just need to ask yourself, what is the worst that can happen? The worst is that one of your jokes will bomb and no one will laugh. So what? No one is going to remember. No one is going to talk about your failed attempt at humor at the water-cooler. You will not end up destitute. The next time you get a chance to speak, try to be funny. As with inventions, the secret to getting more laughs is simply to attempt more jokes. Just remember to keep it clean.

## Recap

- Leverage self-deprecation, exaggerated reality, and challenges to authority to add humor to your talk.

- Embed humor in dialogue.

- 'Riff' on themes with clusters of three, progressively funnier quips to deliver an average of one joke per minute.

# CHAPTER 11

# HOW TO MANAGE YOUR PHYSICAL DELIVERY

**W**hen I first started to develop my public speaking ability, my greatest weakness was that I did not know what to do with my hands. When I consulted reference materials, I either heard useless generalizations (do what comes naturally) or read lists of what not to do. I yearned for something or someone to tell me what ideal physical delivery looks like.

To be comfortable with what do with your arms when not gesturing, just do what you do when you are having a conversation with somebody you trust. When people speak to one another, their rest position is to have their hands comfortably down at their sides. This is the most effective base position in public speaking.

Rather than hands down comfortably at their sides with elbows slightly bent, many people believe that the correct base position is to keep their hands above the waist at all times. Some people put their hands together, some people keep them apart. You can most certainly be a good speaker if you do this, but it is just a bit unnatural. Imagine walking around all day, every day like this. It would be neither comfortable nor confident. Remember, you would never have a conversation with a person whom you care about with your hands up the entire time, because it creates a barrier. Even at a distance, you will be creating the same barrier with your audience. Whatever rest position you choose, make sure that you are able to maintain symmetry; otherwise your nervous tension will become obvious to the audience.

Though many rest positions are acceptable, there are some that you should definitely avoid:

- Fig leaf: Holding your arms down but with your hands coupled in front suggests that you are timid.

- Pockets: Hands in pockets makes you appear passive or disinterested.

- Parade rest: Holding your arms down but with your hands coupled in back suggests that you are hiding something.

- Hips: Hands on hips makes you appear defiant.

- Crossed arms: Crossing your arms is a negative, challenging position.

Next, you want to make natural gestures above the waist, but below the neck. Unless you are acting out a nervous, self-conscious character in a story, avoid touching your face, head, hair, and the back of your neck. For about half the population, hand gestures are a natural part of the way they converse. If you fit into that group, just keep doing what you are doing. If you are in the other half like me, then you are going to have to force yourself to make hand gestures lest you stand uncomfortably fixed like a soldier. It is going to feel awkward initially, but I promise your discomfort will disappear in no time. The only difference between what you do with your arms in normal conversation versus what you do in public speaking is that you should scale your hand gestures up to suit the size of the room. The bigger your audience, the more dramatic your gestures need to be for people to see them.

Effective hand gestures serve to amplify and support, not overwhelm your story. They should be noticeable neither for their presence nor their absence. Occasionally you will see speakers repeat the same gesture to the point where it becomes distracting. Though the majority of your gestures should be above the waist and below the neck, you can add variety by occupying the sphere that surrounds you. In context, it is perfectly acceptable to reach to the heavens or to dig into the depths of the Earth. When people get nervous, they tend to protect themselves by locking their elbows at their sides. Set your arms free.

When you were a child, your mother likely taught you that pointing shows bad manners. However, many presenters forget this rule applies when speaking to an audience as well. Pointing is aggressive if not offensive. What happens if you desperately need to point? There are two nice alternatives. The first is fist-thumb pointing. Just make a fist with your pinky parallel to the floor and your thumb aimed toward your audience and resting on top of your index finger. This is a good technique to use, sparingly, when making an emphatic point. A friendlier but subtler alternative to finger pointing is the palm-up thrust. To execute this one start with your elbow bent and your palm facing upward then extend your arm toward the audience.

Effective use of your arms is just one component of physical delivery. Another is projecting positive body language. For starters, you should shower your audience with a genuine smile. Smiles not only communicate calm confidence but also build trust between you and your audience. Of course, you cannot smile all the time. Make sure that your facial expressions are synchronized with your message. Though there are many aspects to positive body language, the most important factor beyond your smile is your ability to keep your body square and balanced. Face your audience, keeping your shoulders square with your feet planted shoulder width apart. One final tip; after you ask questions, pause and nod to acknowledge your audience's unspoken thoughts. This will sustain a two-way dialogue even though your audience cannot respond verbally.

Once you master your smile and your stance, you must develop your eye-contact skills. The key to being expert at eye-contact is to imagine that you are having a series of conversations with individual audience members lasting for the duration of one sentence or one thought. Doing so will prevent you from scanning the audience or staring at the floor or ceiling. This means locking eye contact for three to five seconds with individuals in a random pattern around the room. By the end of your talk, you should strive to talk to everybody at least once. Make sure that your body is completely facing the individual you are speaking to and look them in the eye, not the eyes. Though I have not seen scientific proof, some speaking coaches recommend looking a person in the left pupil when making an emotional plea and looking them in the right pupil when making a logical argument. The rationale is that the right side of the brain controls emotions but processes images from the left eye, and vice versa. If that is too out there or too much to handle, just pick an eye, any eye, and stick to it. In very large settings, you may divide the room into four or more sections and spend as long as one to three minutes speaking to the section as if it were an individual.

To add variety to eye contact, there is great power in closing your eyes for brief periods. This is appropriate, for example, when you are reminiscing. TED speaker Jill Bolte Taylor uses this technique very effectively at several points in her talk.

You can transform yourself into a true professional through the use of effective movement. Your goal is to make your movement fluid and natural while still retaining discipline. Move with purpose, not simply for variety. Free yourself from the tyranny of the lectern and the screen.

Making this concrete, I recommend that you view the space you have as a theatrical stage with defined and consistent locations for the different parts of your speech. If you are telling a story, then your characters should occupy fixed physical locations. If you are explaining a timeline, then start at your audience's left and work your way to their right. Note that moving toward your audience is a powerful technique for emphasizing key points and for establishing a deeper personal connection.

Remain in one spot with your body and feet pointing towards your audience as you make a point. Then pause and move on transitions. Once you have stopped, begin speaking again. Rather than being awkward, this pause gives your audience time to process your last point and to prepare for your next one. Of course there are times when you may wish to travel a longer distance. In those instances, you can speak while moving. However, when you get to your new position make sure to stop and square up your body so that you do not appear to be wandering or pacing.

In his TEDGlobal 2009 talk, author and former political speechwriter Daniel Pink showed what great movement looks like. The central theme of his talk was to convince businesses to shift their focus from extrinsic rewards to intrinsic incentives to motivate knowledge workers. To support his point, Mr. Pink described an experiment conducted by Princeton University scientist Sam Glucksberg. Here is how Daniel Pink set the stage literally and figuratively:

*"He gathered his participants. And he said, 'I'm going to time you. How quickly can you solve this problem?' To one group he said, 'I'm*

*going to time you to establish norms, averages for how long it typically takes someone to solve this sort of problem.'*

*To the second group he offered rewards. He said, 'If you're in the top 25 percent of the fastest times, you get five dollars. If you're the fastest of everyone we're testing here today, you get 20 dollars.'"*

When he uttered "To one group he said…", Mr. Pink moved to his left and gestured to his left. When he said "To the second group he offered…", he took three giant steps to his right and gestured to the right. Through dialogue, movement, and gestures, Daniel Pink brought the experiment to life in the room with sections of the audience as symbolic study participants.

Another critical stylistic tip to bear in mind is that you are on stage any time your audience can see you. Your manner of dress, grooming, and conduct should be consistent with your message. In addition to the rapport building that you do before the presentation, your performance includes everything you do from the moment you stand up from your chair to the time you sit down. Walk tall when coming and going, and if the situation warrants, smile liberally.

## Recap

- Starting with hands down comfortably at your sides, make natural gestures above the waist and below the neck.

- Synchronize your facial expressions with your message.

- Hold eye contact with individuals for three to five seconds.  In larger settings, engage sections for one to three minutes.

# CHAPTER 12

# HOW TO CREATE VISUALS THAT INSPIRE

When most people think about TEDTalks, they conjure images of elegant, image-rich slide design. While that is certainly true, the best choice you can make in a presentation is to have no slides at all. In fact, four of the ten most viewed TED presenters used no slides in their talks. This includes Ken Robinson, record holder for the highest viewed talk.

If you absolutely, positively need to do something visual, drawing a simple picture is a fantastic alternative to using slides. My personal favorite example from the TED universe is Simon Sinek's TEDxPugetSound presentation from 2009. At exactly two minutes into his eighteen minute talk, Simon walks to a flip chart, picks up a marker, and draws his famous Golden Circle. Imagine a target with three concentric circles. "WHY" is in the bull's eye. "HOW" is in the middle circle. In the outer circle is "WHAT." This simple drawing illustrates how great leaders inspire and how exceptional companies thrive. You do not need to be a great artist to pull this off. Just make your drawing simple, obvious, and legible.

If speaking without a safety net is not your thing and drawing is not an option, then yes, you can use slides in your presentation. Keep in mind that the slides are for the benefit of your audience, not gigantic crib notes for you. Assuming you have the money and the stakes are high, you might want to consider using a world-class presentation designer like Duarte Design or Garr Reynolds of Presentation Zen fame. If you cannot afford their services, at least buy and devour their amazing books.

In the best TEDTalks that do employ slides, you will find three distinct design approaches. They are known by their popular names as the "Godin Method", the "Takahashi Method", and the "Lessig Method." Though you can be a purist and stick to just one approach in your presentation, I recommend blending two or even three to add contrast and variety.

Remember to avoid clipart at all costs and minimize the use of builds, animation, and video since all of these practices take attention away from you.

Entrepreneur and marketing visionary Seth Godin is widely credited with evangelizing the use of image rich slides. Mr. Godin has spoken at two TED events including TED2003 and TED2009. To apply the "Godin Method", fill an entire slide with a fully licensed photograph of sufficiently high resolution. A nice trick is to have the photograph bleed off the page, thus prompting the audience to use their imagination to complete the picture. Using your own photos is certainly an option. However, it can be difficult to find the perfect photo in your vast, untagged personal photo library. An excellent alternative is to purchase royalty-free images from vendors such as iStockPhoto, Corbis, Getty Images, fotolia, or Shutterstock Images. iStockPhoto, in particular, has a consumer friendly interface and consumer friendly pricing.

These photo services offer images in a variety of sizes and file formats which can be a little daunting to the uninitiated. The simple rule of thumb is to match the photo size to the resolution of your projector in pixels. If you have an SVGA projector, then 800 x 600 is sufficient. Mainstream projectors today deliver XGA resolution at 1024 x 768. Better projectors provide SXGA resolution at 1280 x 1024.

Sometimes image sizes are represented with inches and dpi's (dots per inch). You can treat a dpi as a pixel and simply multiply the inches by the dpi to get the image resolution. For example, a 10 inch by 7.5 inch image at 120 dpi would be 1200 x 900 which is sufficient for displaying on a 1024 x 768 XGA projector. Larger images are a waste of money and storage space since you cannot project more pixels than your projector's maximum resolution. As for file format, stick with JPEG/JPG which provides the right tradeoff of size and quality for photographic images. PNG is a decent second choice but avoid GIF (too low quality) and BMP (too bloated).

The second TED-worthy slide design approach available to you is the "Takahashi Method". Named for Japanese computer programmer Masayoshi Takahashi, this method simply requires you to build slides with a few words of very large text. It is a design enlightened update to the very inelegant 7x7 rule. The 7x7 rule calls for creating slides with no more than seven bullets and no more than seven words per bullet. In comparison to a lot of slides out there, 7x7 is a dramatic improvement. However, it is too amateur for a TED presentation where bullet points are frowned upon.

The "Lessig Method" is a hybrid of the "Godin Method" and the "Takahashi Method". As you have probably guessed, it involves blending a full screen image with very simple text.

For example, if you have a person or an animal looking up and to the right in the image, you should place text in their line of sight.

Regardless of which method you use, the most critical rule of graphic design that applies to slide building is "less is more." Be generous with whitespace. Strive for individual slides to be simple and elegant and for the entire deck to form one harmonious whole. For starters, use the minimum possible number of words or directly relevant graphics that you need to get your point across. Again, your voice will be the soundtrack providing additional detail. Minimalism extends to limiting the number of fonts, colors, and images used.

Minimalism also applies to concept density. Great slides have only one "so-what" message. If you have a slide with two pie charts, then split it into two slides. Professional speaking coach Craig Valentine offers a great guideline: "Use slides as a place where you take off and land." Nothing more.

Most designers employ just a single font in a design. Since many slides have titles or short key headline style messages, your best choice is a variant of Helvetica, including its cousin Ariel. Every font carries an emotional context and you should strive to match the typeface to your message. For Helvetica, the mood is neutral yet authoritative – hence a good choice for most presentations. Nearly every sign you see and company logo you come across is constructed with this font.

If you want or need to use multiple fonts, the best advice is to stay within the same family. Beyond size, fonts vary in thickness (light, regular, and bold), as well as other attributes such as italics. All of these variations, in addition to the sparing use of a different font color, will provide contrast. However, you are bound to run into a rare special circumstance where you need something even more starkly different. In that case, you need to dive just a little into the technical details of fonts.

Helvetica is a sans-serif font, meaning that the ends of the characters do not have little semi-decorative lines. If you wish to mix Helvetica with another family, it is best to do so with a serif font or a script font to make the contrast look intentional and not accidental. While sans-serif fonts like Helvetica are great for headlines, a serif font such as Times New Roman is more commonly used for longer passages of text since the little details help quickly guide the eye. Consequently, if you look closely at most advertisements, you will see Helvetica for titles and Times New Roman for body text. Maybe it is not clever or creative, but it is everywhere because it works and is an excellent choice for the rest of us. The mood for Times New Roman is credible and classic. If you need bold contrast, then you can (again, very judiciously) use a script font. I recommend Lucilda Calligraphy which conveys the air of elegant handwriting.

The "less is more" rule also applies to the use of color. Choose a limited palette of at most five colors. To maintain consistency among images, fonts, and backgrounds, an excellent practice is to draw the colors from an image or set of images in the presentation. Many of the most effective palettes are actually monochromatic where the color (hue) stays the same, but the lightness/darkness (tone or value) and brightness/dullness (saturation) vary. Alternatively, you can go for subtle but clear contrast with an analogous color scheme - one in which colors are adjacent on a color wheel. For bold contrast, to be used sparingly, employ complementary colors that sit on opposite sides of the color wheel.

You should also be thoughtful about the colors used in slide backgrounds and foreground. As a general rule, use cool colors such as blue, green, or silver for backgrounds and warm colors like red, yellow, and orange for foregrounds. Neutral colors like black and white may also be suitable for backgrounds. When presenting data, use a solid color that does not interfere with the message.

In addition to the "less is more" philosophy, another set of principles worth internalizing regards attentive placement of text and images. Again, this is the stuff of design community battles, but I recommend that you apply the Rule of Thirds. Just divide a slide into a three-by-three grid of nine equal sized boxes, using this grid to align both text and images. It is perfectly acceptable, and accepted, for elements to span multiple boxes, but do so with awareness and intention. For example, imagine that you consumed an entire slide with a single nature photograph. In that case, you would align the horizon with one of the two horizontal grid lines. If the sky is dull, align it with the top one. If dramatic, then align the horizon with the bottom grid line.

The grid is your guide to where the focal points are on the slide. There are five of them. The first four are at the intersections of the grid lines and make excellent places to place an image. The fifth one is more subtle and is at the visual center of the slide just up and to the right of true center.

**Recap**

- Give your talk with no slides at all.

- Produce simple, image-rich, text-light slides if you must create them.

- Emphasize key points using sparing and intentional contrast in color, font, or placement.

# CHAPTER 13

# HOW TO OVERCOME YOUR FEAR

F ear of public speaking is real and universal. Classifying it as rational or irrational does not make it go away. Knowing that many other people view public speaking as a fate worse than death does not help either. Here are a few valuable and easy tips that will help you manage your fear.

Controlling public speaking anxiety actually begins with what you do long before the day of your presentation. In particular, if you are giving a TEDTalk, you should practice in a feedback rich environment a minimum of three times. A single expert speaker qualifies as a feedback rich environment though you may wish to gather a small group of your friends and peers. Practicing multiple times will give you familiarity and confidence with your content. Since your goal should be to speak conversationally, avoid memorizing or reading off a script.

Your fear will likely intensify when you arrive at your venue. Public speaking is a performance that you are giving for your audience. Just as stage directors ensure that everything is ready before the curtain comes up on a play, great presenters take control of their environment. You must arrive early so that you have adequate time to assimilate or modify the technology and physical space.

If you are using technology, leave no stone unturned. Test your microphone. Run through your slides in presentation mode to ensure the computer is functioning and that graphics are displaying as expected. It is easy to fall into complacency. Once, I inserted a graphic of an innocent enough stop sign into a presentation and did not perform a dry run. To my shock and horror, the stop sign began flashing obnoxiously in a presentation before the senior leadership of my company. Fortunately, they had a sense of humor, but I learned that you can never be too careful.

Understanding and even changing your environment is just as important as testing the technology. Regardless of whether or not you can alter your environment, you should take the time to plan how you will use the physical space. For example, if you have the freedom to move around while speaking, you can determine where to stand and which pathways to take. If you can alter the environment, you might choose to reconfigure chairs and tables, add or remove a podium, or reposition a moveable whiteboard.

Arriving early to gain control of the environment will give you confidence that will carry over into your presentation. However, there is yet another compelling benefit. Once you have mastered the technology and the physical space, arriving early gives you a golden opportunity to build rapport with your audience before you speak. By listening carefully, you will create allies and be able to draw their insights and stories into your speech.

As you start your actual presentation, remember that the audience wants you to succeed. Though I do not recommend memorizing your entire presentation, you should memorize your introduction. When you start strong, your confidence will carry forward. A great tip is to keep the outline of your speech in your pocket. Though you will probably never need it, just knowing it is there gives you an added boost. If you have your speech down cold and are feeling confident, then follow the practice of professional speakers and empty your pockets completely before taking the stage.

Finally, remember that nervous speakers have a tendency to speak too fast. Slow down and make liberal use of pauses. Pauses give your audience time to catch up with your message and they give you time to take slow, deliberate breaths. (Pauses are also part of the "burst and pause" method cure for the filler word plague discussed earlier.)

**Recap**

- Practice your talk a minimum of three times in a feedback rich environment.

- Arrive early at the venue to gain comfort with the logistics and with the audience.

- Remember that your audience wants you to succeed.

# CHAPTER 14

# STOP READING AND START SPEAKING

While creating this book, I studied TED videos. A lot of TED videos. In the same way that watching a lot of Iron Chef will not make you a gourmet cook, watching a lot of great speakers will not make you a great speaker. Reading a library of books on public speaking will not make you a great speaker either. You need to practice in a feedback rich environment. Go spread your ideas.

CPSIA information can be obtained at www.ICGtesting.com
Printed in the USA
LVOW101617280113

317566LV00017B/855/P